WAS IT A CAT I SAW?

l

Published in paperback in 2022 by Davay

© Isabel Kurczynskyj 2022

ISBN 978-1-7392011-4-2

British Library Cataloguing in Publication Data. A catalogue record for this book is available from the British Library.

Printed in Great Britain.

WAS IT A CAT I SAW?

WRITTEN & ILLUSTRATED BY ISABEL KURCZYNSKYJ

To Horace, Jasper, Tibby, Ben and Lulabell,
and many other brief encounters.

FOREWORD

This illustrated, alphabetical dictionary has been compiled in admiration, intrigue and with a love of cats in a jovial observation of this magnificent species. It's a collection of fun, fictitious words and phrases to describe the innate behaviours and traits.

This first edition only 'scratches' the surface… many more unique words and phrases have been collected locally and from further afield over several years, and will be available in a second illustrated dictionary coming soon.

Baffinator

Momma cat cleaning kitten.

I've never been a hygiene-hater
but a test of that does happen.
Now I've been a mucky kit…
get washed clean by the baffinator.

Belleh Trap

When cats lay on their backs, revealing their fluffy bellehs,
enticing you to touch and stroke. But if you do,
like the Venus Flytrap, they may enclose your hand
in their clawed needle vice and bunny-kick you
until you withdraw…

…if possible.

Bitey-face

*When kittens target each others faces
by biting in play fights.*

Blep

A tongue protrusion.

Meh aah mo murds (you twy!)

Catermelon

A heavily pregnant queen.

Waddle and sway,
kitten watch is on…
momma cat to be
is a catermelon.

Catting (prefixed with 'great' or 'top').

Cats doing audacious and cheeky stuff.

Our job and our nine lives ambition,
make no attempt at combatting
to tip, trip and cavort,
everyone knows is great catting.

Clickety-purr

The sound of the developing purr of a kitten, particularly audible when new-borns are suckling.

Crab puff

When kittens/cats arch their back,
fluff out their fur and walk sideways.

Be afraid, I might be in a huff,
showing I'm strong and tough
with my broadside fluffy crab puff.

Derp

Stopping suddenly when licking,
leaving the tip of tongue out.

Caught off-guard in mid-slurp,
the protrusion forgotten
is called a derp.

Elevator Butt

When a cat stands and lowers its front half and at the same time stretches and extends its back legs higher in response to strokes and scritches along its lower back and near the base of their tail, sometimes making biscuits at the same time which sometimes involves all four paws.

Fluffy Peanuts

The shape of new-born kittens.

Gackens

Cat vomiting.

It's not always fur-balls, or a breakfast seconds,
it also happens in the dead of night
on your slippers, preforming gackens!

Groot (to groot)

Lay flat on back with front legs above head.

Laying flat-out like this,
I think I might take root,
flat as a pancake,
raised to the ground,
this pose is called a groot.

Gushies

When it's time to introduce kittens
to solid foods, kitten food is mixed with
kitten milk or water to make a slurry.

Kittens don't eat special foods
like caviar or sushies…
Coz when we're very little,
we much prefer the gushies.

Handicat

A cat with a disability.

Sometimes we're born like that,
Sometimes it's a mishap…
but nothin' ever stops us,
we is mighty Handicat.

If I fits, I sits

To perch upon or climb into boxes, freshly laundered clothing,
computer keyboards, plant pots, sinks, open drawers…

As every cat and felid knows,
an impulse we can't resist…
whatever the size or shape of it,
if I fits, I sits.

Jet-ears

When cats retract and flatten their ears
to protect from threat or sometimes to hear
a sound coming from behind.

Kitty Croissant

When a cat or kitten curls themselves tightly,
normally when asleep on their side.

The French word 'impuissance',
a feeling of tired or weak,
I curl up and go fast asleep
and become a kitty croissant –
et c'est 'purr'quoi.

Kitty-quake

Fast body twitches when sleeping.

When fastest asleep,
nothing stirs me awake,
My body does a kitty-quake.

Loaf/loafing

When a cat sits with all their paws
tucked underneath their body.

There was no yeast,
I promise on oath,
Beneath my legs are neatly tucked,
And now I am a loaf.

Making biscuits

*The motion of kittens' front paws that starts
at suckling stage and generally remains as a comfort,
excitement or contentment action throughout adulthood.*

Mewcopter

When cats do a rapid side to side head-shake.

Milkbar

A nursing momma cat.

I have my favourite flavour at milky time,
so push and shove at the milkbar,
and although I love my siblings dearly,
I wish I had a crowbar!

Mood Noodle

The tail.

I cannot read, write or doodle,
I exhibit my feelings
with my mood noodle.

Moggos

A name not just for doggos!

Niptinis

The intoxication-like effects of catnip.

There is a hero who likes Martinis,
but cats don't grapple with villains…
we much prefer to roll about,
after a few Niptinis.

Opiniows

A cat vocalising an (always) important message.

Panfur

A black cat.

Despite the fables about luck or not,
there's more to us than superstition…
so please do take a closer look,
and just delete the 'stition'.

Spigot

Nipple, as in kitten latching onto a spigot.

Push, shove, elbow and pivot,
I must to latch onto my favourite spigot.

Spock Ear

The occasional times when cat ears (painlessly)
backward fold… they generally spring back
on their own after a few moments.

We have two pointy things
that pivot around to hear…
when we paw too hard,
when washing them clean,
we end up with Spock ear!

Stinky-face

A Flehmen response induced by the sniffing of
a pheromone laden or other scent of interest.
The pupils enlarge and the mouth partially opens
and remains ajar. An expression of intense concentration
and thought ensues which lasts a few seconds.
Felids and a range of other animals also do this.

If I'm distracted by something that froze my pace,
to process the scent my nose detected,

I display my stinky-face…

Tortitude

Cats with Calico or Tortie markings are sometimes thought to be gifted with a feisty and headstrong demeanour.

Tree-flappers

Loose leaves cats like to chase on a breezy day.
Breezes often evokes a zoomie too.

Weansie

A cat 'onesie' that is sometimes worn by a nursing momma cat during the time kittens are transitioning to eating solid foods.

(See also gushies).

Whappy-paws

*Kittens pushing each other with their front paws
to get to a 'spigot' at the 'milkbar'.*

I have a favourite spigot, I have it early doors,
but if I wake up late and it's been had,

I activate whappy-paws!

Zoomies

When cats run at speed, in short spurts, in all and any direction.